Kitchen Utensils

Mike Wheeler and David Byrne

This book looks at the scientific ideas behind some common kitchen tools and machines. It also gives scientific reasons for choosing cooking utensils made of particular materials.

If you are using the book to find out p_____ about kitchen utensils, you do not have to read it all. ____ **ontents** (below) or the **index** (at the back) to f_____ _____ ages to help you. Then just read as much as you nee__

The basic facts are given in big print, and _____ ___ed information is in smaller print.

Contents

1 Materials in the kitchen

In the kitchen it is important that some equipment gets hot quickly. Some other equipment has to stay cool.

Saucepans are often used to heat up food, so pans have to be made from materials that get hot quickly. The handles do not get hot easily.

↥ The pan gets hot quickly and heats the beans.

Some parts of the saucepans should not get hot.

Conductors and insulators

Conductors are materials that allow heat to pass through them. Saucepans are made from materials that conduct heat so that they get hot. Steel, copper and glass are all good conductors. This allows the food to heat up quickly.

The handles of saucepans do not get hot. This is because they are made from materials that do not allow heat to pass through. Materials that do not allow heat to pass through them are called insulators. Wood, plastics and some fabrics are good insulators. Handles of saucepans are made of insulators so that the pan can be picked up safely.

Using conductors and insulators

Conductors and insulators of heat can be found all around a kitchen. Oven gloves are used to remove hot pans from the oven. The fabric of the gloves acts as an insulator because it has air trapped within the fibres. This air traps the heat inside it and does not allow the heat to pass through.

▲ Oven gloves insulate your hands from the heat.

Pans, baking trays, frying pans and ovenproof dishes are all examples of kitchen tools made from materials that are conductors of heat. When they are placed on a hot ring of electricity or gas, or placed in a hot oven, this material allows heat to pass through them. Heat likes to move from hot places to cooler places so that it is spread evenly. The heat slowly cooks the food.

Be careful not to burn or scald yourself when you are using the oven. Always use oven gloves.

Activity

Take a jug and fill it with water which is hot (not boiling!). Stand a large metal spoon and a wooden spoon in the jug for about five minutes.

When you feel the two spoons, you will notice that the handle of the metal spoon is warm. This is because the heat has been conducted from the hot water.

Be careful not to burn or scald yourself with hot water.

 Metal conducts heat and wood does not conduct heat.

2 Machines in the kitchen

A lot of work is done in the kitchen.
To help us in our work, we use machines.
Machines make work easier. They give us more time
to do what we want.

Machines in the kitchen help us do things more quickly and easily.

Food mixers, dishwashers and microwave ovens are all examples of machines that can be found in a kitchen. They all help us to do things more easily.

Not all machines are complicated. Kitchen tools such as a spoon, a fork, a knife or a whisk allow us to do things more easily. A spoon helps us take an egg out of boiling water safely. A fork or a whisk allows us to beat an egg white until it is fluffy.

A whisk can be used to beat eggs. ➡➡

 A fork and knife helps this girl to cut up her food and carry it to her mouth.

7

Energy is used in different machines

Machines need energy to work. In the kitchen, energy comes mainly from people, electricity or gas.

Machines in the kitchen very often use levers, wedges, gears or motors to transfer energy in a way that makes them work for us.

lever   This lever increases the force from our hands.
The energy comes from people.

wedge   The sharp wedge of the knife concentrates the force from our hand and splits the cabbage open.
The energy comes from people.

8

gear   These gears help us to whisk up a mixture quickly and easily.
The energy comes from people.

motor   The electric motor turns the drum and pumps the water.
The energy comes from electricity.

Activity

Look at all the hand tools in your kitchen. Can you find levers, gears and wedges?

9

3 More complicated machines

There are many machines
to be found in a kitchen.
Some machines work by hand.

Other machines work by
using electricity.
Many electrical machines
have motors.

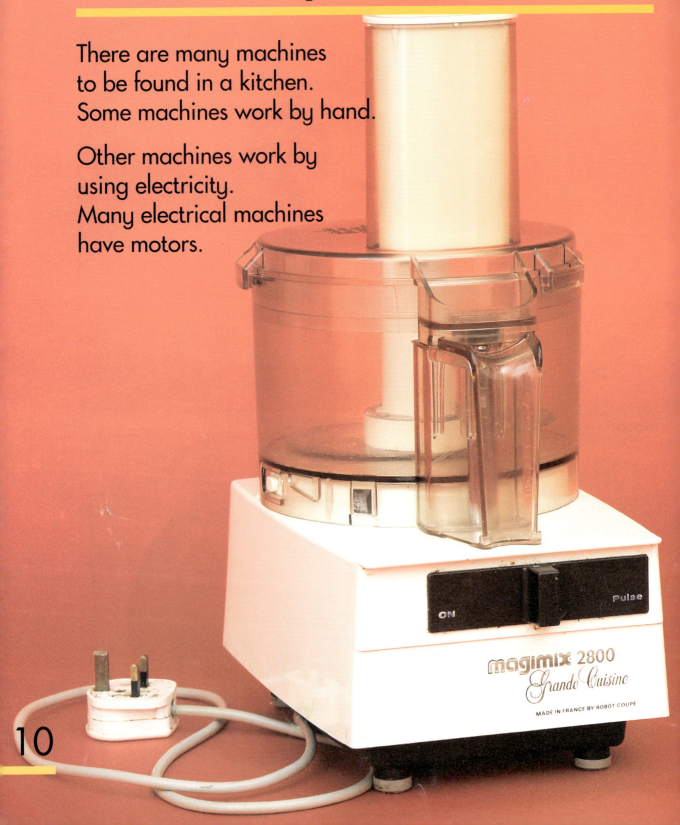

magimix 2800
Grande Cuisine

MADE IN FRANCE BY ROBOT COUPE

In the kitchen there are simple machines and complicated machines. Simple machines have only one or two moving parts. A knife, a pair of scissors or a nutcracker are examples of simple machines.

Complicated machines have many different moving parts. Examples of a complicated machine include a hand whisk and an electric whisk.

Complicated machines use moving parts to transfer energy from one place to another. These moving parts include pulleys and gears. A pulley has wheels joined together by a belt. Gears are wheels with teeth which mesh together to transfer movement.

 The inside of an electric whisk. You can see the gears which move the whisk.

Machines and energy

All machines need some sort of energy to make them work. The simple machines in a kitchen often use human energy, whilst the complicated machines often use electrical energy. Electrical energy can easily be changed into movement, heat, light or sound. It will turn a motor which will make a machine work.

An electric food mixer uses gears to transfer movement energy from its motor to the moving part, either a whisk or a blade.

Pulleys and gears are used in machines to control the speed and direction of the movement.

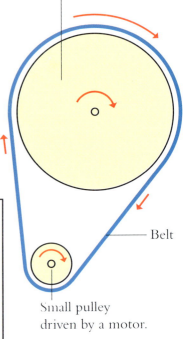

Large pulley which moves the washing machine tub.

Belt

Small pulley driven by a motor.

A diagram of a washing machine tub.

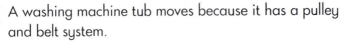
A washing machine tub moves because it has a pulley and belt system.

Activity

Take a handmixer and turn the handle
around once. Count the number of times
that the beaters revolve. You will notice
that they turn more times than the handle.
Can you explain why?

4 Kitchen knives

A knife is a simple tool used to cut and chop many things in the kitchen. The blades of kitchen knives are often made of steel, and the handles made of wood or plastic. There are different knives for different jobs.

bread knife

carving knife

meat knife

dinner knife

vegetable knives

A kitchen knife works when it is pulled backwards and forwards across the surface of food. There must be movement, coupled with a gentle push from the hands, for a knife to cut. When the blade of the knife is sharp it cuts through food very easily, but this can be very dangerous.

The handles of knives are shaped to help you hold them safely. They are usually made from a material which protects and insulates your hand from the heat. The blade is often pointed so that it can be used as a lever.

You must always ask for the help of an adult when you use sharp kitchen knives.

Knives for the job

A knife can do different jobs, using force in lots of directions – for cutting, scooping, lifting, slicing etc. A machine that can do this is called a force multiplier. Knives can be designed in many ways to carry out different tasks around the kitchen.

A bread knife
The serrated edge improves the action of the blade.

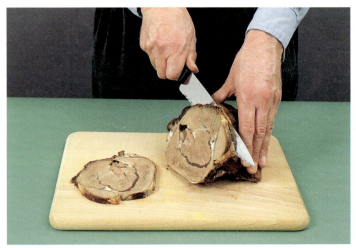

A grapefruit knife
The curved, serrated blade is used to cut round the curved skin of the fruit, and separate it from the flesh.

A meat knife
The sharp, strong and straight blade allows you to apply a lot of force.

A fish knife

The flat blade allows you to lift fish off the bones.

A child's knife

Knives can be designed to fit all sizes of hand.

An electric knife

Electricity can move the blade so that it cuts easily.

You must always ask for the help of an adult when you use sharp kitchen knives.

17

5 Scissors

Scissors are often used in the kitchen to help us to cut things.
Scissors are made of two parts which are joined together. We use our fingers and thumb to push the two parts together. The pushing makes the scissors cut.

You must always ask for the help of an adult when using sharp scissors.

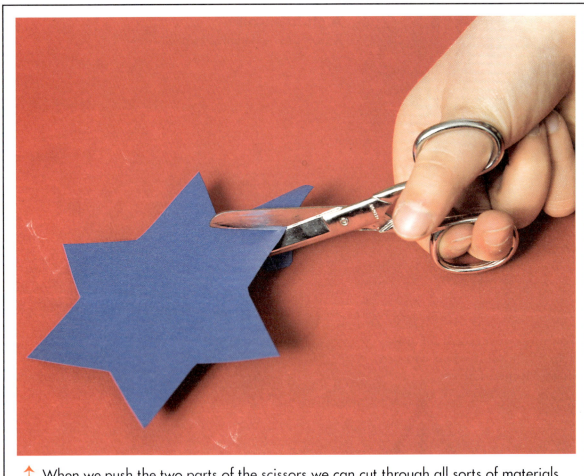

When we push the two parts of the scissors we can cut through all sorts of materials.

 Scissors are very useful in the kitchen.

Scissors are a simple machine. There are two stiff blades which are held together by a rivet or a screw.

The blades are attached to handles which allow you to work the scissors with your fingers and thumb. When you push the handles together, the blades close and they cut into the material between them.

The blades are narrower at the cutting edge. This helps to increase the effect of the push that you put into the handles.

Scissors can be very dangerous, and you should always be careful when you use them.

Applying force by design

Scissors are designed to do work for us. They make the force from our hands act better. In a pair of scissors there are two types of simple machine that are operating, called the lever and the wedge.

The lever in scissors

A lever is a stiff shape which can lift, cut or move objects easily by pivoting upon a turning point. This turning point is called a fulcrum.

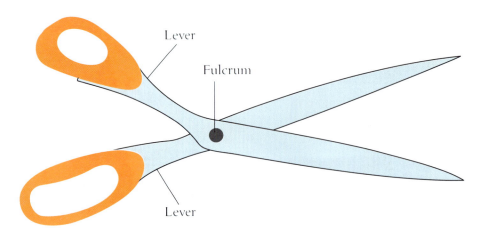

Lever

Fulcrum

Lever

The wedge in scissors

A wedge is a simple machine with a thin edge. If a force is applied to it, it will concentrate the effect of the force at the thin edge and cut through the material. As the edge cuts into the material, the wider part of the wedge pushes the material apart.

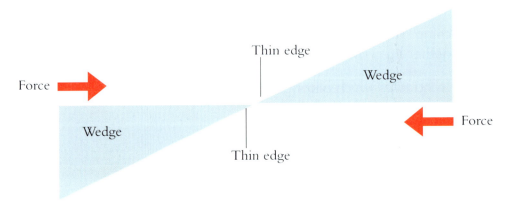

Thin edge

Wedge

Force

Wedge

Force

Thin edge

The fulcrum in scissors

The use of a pair of scissors can be changed by altering its design. If the distance between the point at which the force is applied and the fulcrum is increased, then the scissors can cut more effectively.

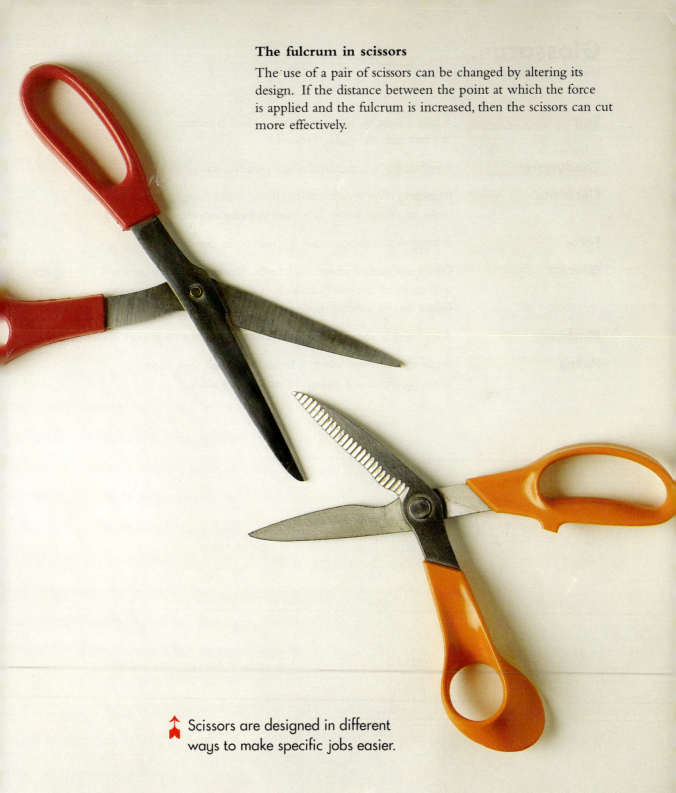

Scissors are designed in different ways to make specific jobs easier.

21

Glossary

Belt

A belt is used by some machines to turn a pulley.
The belt pulls the pulley around.

Conductors

A conductor is a material which gets hot easily.

Electricity

Electricity is an invisible force. It can make things get hot, light up,
make sounds or move. It is used to make many machines work.

Force

A force makes things move by pushing or pulling them.

Gears

Gears are special wheels with teeth. The teeth on one gear will join together
with teeth on another gear to turn it. A hand whisk uses gears.
Gears can be used to speed a machine up or slow it down.

Machine

A machine is something built by people to make their work easier to do.

Pulley

A pulley is a wheel which is turned by a belt (See above).
Some machines use pulleys to make them work.

Further information

Books

Kitchens now and long ago by Sallie Purkis, Longman, 1994.
This book tells about kitchens in history including some of the equipment used.

At Home

Look in your kitchen at home to see if you have any of the machines
mentioned in the book.

Do you have any other machines in your kitchen?
Are they simple or complicated?

Index

a b c d e f g h i j k l m n o p q r s t u v w x y z
A B C D E F G H I J K L M N O P Q R S T U V W X Y Z